Pillow Thoughts II
Healing the Heart

Pillow Thoughts II
Healing the Heart

Courtney Peppernell

Andrews McMeel
PUBLISHING®

Acknowledgments

I would like to thank my support system—James, Emma, Rhian, my family, my pups Hero and Dakota, Kirsty Melville, Patty Rice, and the team at Andrews McMeel Publishing for believing in me and helping to bring my words to life. I believe we are always right where we are meant to be, so it's an honor to have amazing people be a part of this journey.

Twitter: @CourtPeppernell
Instagram: @Courtneypeppernell
Email: courtney@pepperbooks.org

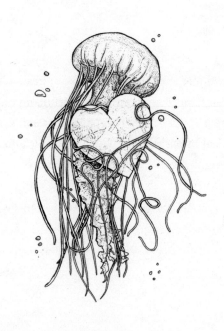

Before we begin, I'd like to remind you of a story.
Once upon a time, there was a jellyfish called
You.
You had been lost
You had been a little unsure
You tried very hard
and You began to heal.
Now You must remind others that sometimes
hearts ache.
I hate to spoil the ending
But You
can heal hearts.

Table of Thoughts

If your heart is in love

Love is all around us.
It's in flowers and sunsets,
it's the whisper in trees,
the breath of a newborn child.
It's two teenage lovers, free and wild.
Love is a mountain, a river, a hand to hold,
it's courageous, fierce, honest, and bold.
It's a shoulder when you weep,
a blanket when you sleep.
It is family, it is strength, it is faith.
Love has no boundaries, no gender,
love just exists.

You shouldn't lose sleep over somebody any more than they should lose sleep over you. But you do, we all do.

And we call this love.

Jealousy will be a part of every relationship. You cannot run from it because it will always exist. But do talk about it; your feelings are valid and shouldn't be dismissed.

You have every right to love your solitude
Being alone doesn't always mean you are lonely

I am a solar system

with crashing comets and star clusters

And in all my pieces

she exists

I can feel her so strongly

it's like I am not even me

anymore

Like all my pieces belong to her

I know life isn't always about bright colors and fireworks. Sometimes the colors aren't always clear, and our days get so hard they hurt. But settle down with me, hold my hand, let me kiss you. All I want is to know you more.

Better than anyone else has before.

Love won't always give you the answers you are looking for.

But you need to come to peace with it anyway.

Even if you never know why, even if after everything, it was easier to say goodbye.

I spend half the morning thinking about your phone call, and when we were up all night talking. How I felt the effect of your words on my heart. I lie in bed and I think of you. I know you come with baggage, but so do I. I know you're scared because of how others treated you. But as the sun rises and sets, I'm falling in love with all the things you do.

A Wedding Gift

I know two people and they are in love.

He is charming and tall, she is beautiful and strong.

Together I wish them happiness, to last a lifetime that is long.

I wish them all the good things in life

that remind them to be humble and kind.

I wish them success and adventures

and to leave all their troubles behind.

Dearest friends, may you today be man and wife

and live with love for the rest of your life.

Sometimes the smallest details about a person are the biggest reasons why you love them

Hold on to your love

if she is good and pure

Keep her close

and if you dream of her

if you are a magnet to her touch

tell her how in love you are

You can't choose which parts of her you love. Even in all the ugly moments, she should still be the woman you want to spend the rest of your life with. People are not perfect, they have flaws. You don't get to choose which ones to leave out.

That's not honest love.

You always just want more. Longer kisses, longer hugs, more time spent together. You'll drive around the block five times just to keep them another hour. Everything is another story to the bookshelf you are building. Their happiness becomes just as important as yours. You learn to love what they love. You'll want to be better. Because they've made you better.

You are not more than I can handle.
Even if you come with a suitcase full of insecurities,
I will still want to know you.
Even if there are days when you are crying
and don't believe in your worth, I will still want to hold you.
I know you have struggled; so have I.
I know that things are hard on you; me too.
But it doesn't change how big your heart is.
I am old enough to make my own choices, and I choose you.

All these people who come and go

and you are still

the only one

I wish to truly know

I bought a sweater the other day, the same color as your eyes. I started listening to your favorite band, wondering how the music made you feel. I started reading books with characters who reminded me of you. When I caught the train to the city, I wished you were there too. If this is what love feels like, I am seeing you in everything I do.

In the end when we are laughing at our child's wedding, I want to joke, "I don't know how you put up with me for forty years," knowing we'll spend forty more together.

I have messy handwriting and I don't always know what to say, but I would write love letters to you all day. I leave the house without an umbrella in the rain, but I would choose you again and again. I get stuck with too many thoughts in my head, but I listen to every word you've ever said. I can be forgetful and spend nights all over the place, but your name is in my heart and it takes up the most space.

My pen could write

for a thousand people

But it never smiles about them

the way it does for you

I just want to wear your t-shirts and wake up in your arms. I just want to kiss you over coffee and sleep in with you during rainstorms. I just want to hold your hand in the street without having to worry what people will think.

When the sun rises, and you are awake, you are beautiful
I could spend all day connecting the freckles across your back
As long as you will have me, then I will be yours
because I want to make you happy for all our years
So, I want to say thank you for all that you are and do
and my heart is so full of all its love for you

I love this closeness between us. I pine for every one of her kisses. I'd spend my days driving the coastline with my love beside me. An infinite dark sky with stars because she reminds me of the moon. Moments spent with her can never come soon enough. To watch our love grow between white sheets and wine, from strangers to she-is-mine. To be young and wild, then to blossom together into old age. If I could write all my love for her between these lines, it would fill every page.

We are in that funny little stage where we are always together but some nights we are not. But I can't stand those nights alone, because my body wrapped around the curve of your back and the sounds of your breath in the dark are now the only ways I can sleep.

Tonight, we are apart, so I am awake.

Being with her is like listening to a song that I will always remember. It doesn't matter how many times I listen to the song, I'll always remember my first time hearing it. It felt like the song knew me, and not who I pretended to be when the headphones weren't in. It felt like driving around late at night, and the song plays on the radio, and you just know it's a song that will change your life.

We aren't perfect, we never will be. But I love talking to you, I love telling you how I feel and having you listen to me. And I love listening to you too. All your hopes and dreams and insecurities. Because when everything fades away and our age begins to show, all we will have left is to listen. And because I love the sound of your voice and the echoes of your soul, I will listen to you for the rest of your life. Your thoughts mirror my thoughts, together, two parts of a whole.

I daydream about the day you will be my wife. It'll be Christmastime, and our children will be asleep while we are in the living room by the tree, trying to be quiet but giggling over wine. You will still look beautiful in pajamas with your hair past your shoulders, and I'll still love the tree lights even if we are getting older. We will try to guess what our boy and girl will say after they notice the half-eaten cookie and the drop of milk left on the plate and tray. And my heart will flutter as you kiss my lips, and we'll say "Merry Christmas," because life was meant to be just like this.

All you do is smile

and I feel it in my soul

How do you do that?

You make me feel your love

even in my bones

You're incredible

I hope you know

how I love you so

I didn't stand a chance, the minute I saw you across the hall. In the blink of an eye my heart was yours. Now I'm wondering if destiny exists, if fate rests in our hands and makes us fall so in love we can barely stand. I want to know the taste of your lips, and how far I would go to keep you safe. Even if I have loved long before, this time my heart is beating loud. We've been taking photographs to hang up on the wall, of memories and adventures and days lived together, and yet I still remember the moment I saw you across the hall.

There are things we take for granted, like fresh laundry and a window to watch the sky. There are times we see loss and pain and we question why. But I will never apologize for leaning across the passenger seat to press my lips to yours. I will never apologize for telling the world that you are what is important in my life and in my eyes. I will never apologize for starting our days with good mornings and ending them with goodbyes. I will never apologize for all the memories that we share or the lyrics we poorly sing. I will never apologize for all this love I have to give. Because it's yours and I love you more than anything.

We're young, but not that young. Some people are sixty-five and still feel young. Just because we have years ahead of us doesn't mean our love isn't going to last a lifetime. Then again maybe we don't have years; everything could end tomorrow. But I will love you anyway. Every day, deeply, wholeheartedly, even if we are young, even if we are old. My love for you will be gentle, but fierce and bold.

When I am on the subway coming home from work, I think about waking up on a Sunday morning with your side of the bed made. I will dress in sweats and find you in the kitchen, standing by the window with coffee and staring into the yard. The sunlight will be in your hair, and you'll catch me trying not to stare. You will smile, with lips that have me drunk in love, and you'll ask how I slept. And I'll say better than ever, because I felt safe with you, and that's a feeling I want forever.

Tell me how to reach your heart

Show me where you keep it

Let me stay

Maybe that's what life is about,

you wait for that person

who you could listen to for hours.

That person who is going to have

a real conversation with you,

make you laugh,

make you feel a little lost

when you hang up the phone.

You will always be my destination, my home, my whole heart.

I love to love you.

You'll Just Know

You'll see them in everything.

Suddenly the sun reflecting off your windshield glows the same way as their smile. The supermarket reminds you of that Sunday morning they tried to make you pancakes and got flour all over the floor. The blanket at the foot of your bed suddenly becomes a substitute when they're not there, and every single time, it's not nearly warm enough.

Their eyes become galaxies to get lost in. You think they're the funniest, smartest, most beautiful person you have ever met. They drive you crazy in the best way. You're always drunk on the thought of them.

Suddenly their body becomes a map, a diagram, a place to create pathways with your own fingertips. You'll treat this as a delicate rite of passage, as though someone is letting you touch gold. You're an artist who wants to draw across their canvas. You're an explorer who wants to discover all the places your body fits with theirs.

Each hug feels like it's not long enough. When they fold into you. When they hang off every word you say. You smell them everywhere. In your bedsheets, on your clothes, as soon as they walk into the room. They smell like pine oak in the spring, like firewood in the winter, like rain on a summer night.

The way they look at you. The way they spell and say your name.

You know their coffee order, you know what days they do laundry because they'll call you to borrow clothes. You know their favorite color, what makes them laugh, what turns them on, what books they'll read, what movies they'll pick, everything they hate about themselves you'll love even more. You want to see the world with them.

You think about the future. Marrying them. It scares you. It excites you. You don't know whether to think about it, but you can't help it. You think about whether you'll get a cat or dog first. What house you'll have, what your children will look like.

You'll want to be better. Because they've made *you* better.

Above anything, love will always come back into your life.

Love isn't always about falling in love with a person. Love is passing your final exams. Love is watching the sun come up between the clouds. Love is finding the light when you were in the dark. Love is when your favorite TV show returns. Love is when your dog tilts its head with confusion. Love is a free ice cream voucher left on your car windshield. Love is the leaves falling in the fall. Love is learning the constellations. Love is solving a ridiculous math problem. Love is the changing Starbucks menu for the seasons. Love is watching a child play in the sandbox. Love is warm clothes when they come out of the dryer. When you say you've given up on love, all you're really saying is that you've closed your eyes.

Open them.

It is said that artists paint portraits of the ones they love. Well, writers do it too. Only they string together sentences about all the things that might be too hard to say in person. Writers don't just write about nothing. They write about the things kept in the deepest part of their hearts. They write with passion, with meaning. They write to show you that they care. And more than that, they trust you with their words. They give you their words, because they are trying to say "I love you."

I hope you find a love that listens to you when you need to talk. I hope you find a love that never takes you for granted. I hope you find a love that makes you feel safe. I hope you find a love that wishes for your dreams as much as you do. I hope you find a love that kisses you with such intensity, in that moment you forget how to breathe.

If your heart is aching

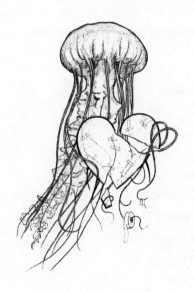

The Three Kinds of Heartbreak

The first is when
someone is reckless with
your heart
and it breaks and shatters
in ways
you never thought it could

The second is when
you break
someone else's heart
Because you'll never
know pain
like the type that has you
look into their eyes
but they look away

And the worst kind of heartbreak
is the kind that comes along
when you have to watch
the person you love
be happy
with someone else

Sometimes heartbreak will feel light, like a feather falling from the sky. Other times it will hurt so much you'll stand in front of the mirror and beg, why? It will come and go through chapters of your life. You will cry. You will lie awake at night hoping it will pass in the morning.

And it will pass.

The ache will pass with every tide and return when things have come crashing down.

It is a continuous cycle, here to make you stronger.

When she puts her arms around you, she will make you feel safe, but rarely will she take you in her arms. She will call you late at night when the radio is playing her favorite song and tell you how much it reminds her of you. But these are the same songs she has dedicated to those before you. Listen to her when she's crying; it's one of the only times she will tell you the truth. She will pretend to understand you, and you'll believe her when she says she loves all your flaws. She will tell you she wants all the same things you do, but she doesn't. She doesn't know what she wants. She will tell you that you are the only thing she needs, but you aren't. She will want others. She will believe she is always right even when she's not and you know she's not, but you'll stop arguing anyway. You'll stay because her selfishness and her recklessness don't seem less than ordinary. Everyone around you will constantly say how beautiful she is, a work of art, someone extraordinary. Until the day she shows the true colors underneath her mask. They will be dark and dangerous and in your hesitation, you might survive. You might just dodge a bullet.

For the person who loves her next, because I couldn't.

My eyes hurt from staring at a screen trying to forget the memories. My legs hurt from running through empty streets trying to forget all the nights you slept in my sheets. My hands hurt from trying to distract myself in the pages of a book. I've been hoping to forget your smile and the way you look.

The static can make our distance

sound like love

When soft words seem

enough

for all the miles in between

I'm sorry for not calling back

I'm sorry for all the nights I disappeared

because things are never as they seem

I dream about you too much

Sometimes I lose myself in those dreams

and I imagine the way you breathe

and if you talk in your sleep

and the way I'd kiss you awake

But then I must remind myself

that you won't be here when I wake up

I guess that's why

I'm afraid of the dark

I wanted to take your breath away

make your heart race

your eyes only for me

But you live life recklessly

in all your lonely space

I wanted to fill parts of you

to love you with all I had

But not if it meant losing myself

in your misery

So now I look the other way

when you pass by

And I've given up

on all our history

Thinking maybe you are

just better left a mystery

I waited on the bridge, but you never came

I waited all day for someone

who I thought felt the same

I'll see you when I see you

I'll still love you when I do

But for now

Goodbye to you

Goodbye to

all the things

I can't keep holding on to

My dreams were always of you
but every time I closed my eyes
you belonged to someone else

It hurt to love her

Days spent wondering if she would get better

But she could not save herself

and I started to realize

we weren't meant to be

    and in the end

        the person I ended up saving

          was me

The hesitation will be quiet. It will come when you least expect it. It will rise from the depths of your aching soul and settle in your heart as three words.

— I deserve better

In the years to come, I hope to be proud of you. I hope that I will not think of all the terrible things you did or the carelessness you showed my heart. I hope your soul will grow and the distance will allow forgiveness to settle in between the spaces that keep us apart. I hope I show empathy for the kindness you lacked, and that time proves its compassion to my old wounds.

Leaving

You handed me the box, and I held on to it for a moment, hoping my feet would move toward the door. But I wanted you to say something, to make everything hurt less. You could have said anything, and I would have been grateful.

The silence hung between us, like a heart slowly breaking. I reached for the door, pulled it open, one foot in the hallway, the other in a home that wasn't ours anymore. It was strange, what you said next, when you turned to me and asked,

"You haven't left anything behind, have you?"

I had laughed, a sad little laugh that traveled from me to you, but only because I knew we were both remembering the same thing. All the times I had left my shoes or coat or wallet at your place and you would call me to let me know. I was constantly returning to collect things. I never told you that I was always leaving things behind so I could return the next day, just to see you again.

But there wouldn't be a next day anymore.

I looked at you one last time, right before stepping through the apartment door, and I hoped in time we would look back with fond memories. But now I realize how sad the last thing you had said to me was. After you closed the door, I *was* leaving something behind again.

It was you.

You will have your heart broken so badly

you will question if love still exists

But there are still souls in this life

who will say your name in between

kisses spelled with their lips

and they will hold your hand

and they won't let go

There is no such thing as heartlessness. If someone is cruel and unkind, it is because they do not know of the kindness from strangers or the light within love. And if they do not know of light, how sad and lonely they must be, to become demons of the night.

Just because the bruises aren't visible doesn't mean they aren't there

The saddest ache you will ever know

is to wake up one day and realize

you have run out of time

Heartbreak isn't always tears and packing away a box of her old things. It can be a highway late at night and thinking about the way she used to sing. It can be an empty aisle in the grocery store, looking at her favorite chocolate and not wanting to buy it anymore.

There is always one who is careful and safe while the other is wild and brave. Together things will get so messy it's hard to want more. And with forgotten memories littered on the floor, one will always have a suitcase packed and a foot out the door.

But you know what it means to be happy

　　When things seem simpler and not piled on

　　　as though you might break

Reaching out for help is never a bad thing

　　We need to be better

　　　Before it's too late

The grief will feel like a shadow. Each time you look in the mirror it will be around you. But its purpose is to guide you back from the depths of despair. It might not make any sense, but grief understands what you can handle.

It knows what is and isn't fair.

As tragic as it seems

as hurtful as it feels

if they gave up on you

in your worst moment

they never really loved you

Just because it hurts doesn't mean you need to shrink your heart into something that can no longer feel. Open your arms with your face to the sky. We were not made to be easy to love. All that soul inside you will still be heard, even after the day you die.

They broke your heart, so you found yourself reading texts and letters to piece together where it all went wrong. You have sleepless nights and thoughts pushing you to the limit. Because heartbreak can also mean a broken spirit.

If you are not happy, you are not obligated to stay. If they want to make you come undone and make you question all that you are worth, then it's best to walk away.

The high school dance will feel like a moment that defined you. That nothing else in life mattered and no one else existed. Until you're older and you've discovered even bones can ache and not everyone will give you a second chance. So, you'll stare into an empty bottle and wish life were as simple as a high school dance.

How many heartbreaks can you survive?

All of them

Because you are not merely

skin and bones

You are the light and wonder

You are a joy to be known

You are the castle a soul calls home

You could beg someone to heal you
in all the ways you can't heal yourself.
But other people are not bandages.
You are your own journey.
The pain belongs to you.

You still love them, even if they no longer love you. There is bravery in letting go of a love you thought you knew. There is no shame in wanting someone who doesn't want you back. But darling, you deserve someone who wants to love you just as much.

Ache is good for you, even though I know it doesn't feel like it at the time. When someone breaks your heart, you can barely move from bed. And you start to question if you were ever good enough. All these messy thoughts inside your head. But your heart needs to break in ways that don't seem fair. It needs to survive someone cruel and selfish and unkind. Because you will learn that life is only meant to be lived with someone who respects your hopes and dreams like their own. Heartbreak teaches you the difference between a person who is no good for you and someone who would never leave you alone.

The hardest thing you will ever do in your life is forgive someone who never apologized. But you don't need to do this for them; you need to do this for yourself.

You are not the only person to be broken, and you won't be the last. There have been centuries of broken hearts, each with their own stories: a future, present, and past. So, you must know that despite the ache in your soul and your shaking voice, there is seldom a heart that escapes pain like it has a choice. But you do get to choose how you recover. And that is something that cannot be taken away from you, not even by another.

Feel it, all of it. The pain, the ache, the voice in your head screaming "Why did you stay for as long as you did?" You are allowed to pity yourself, you are allowed nights where you can barely move from bed. There is no limit on the time it takes to heal. But you must continue to feel. You need to break and bend and then ask yourself when all the misery will end. Because it will end. One morning you will wake up and you will notice the sun, you will notice the newspaper on your front lawn and that the nightmares have gone, you will notice yourself and how far you've come in moving on.

I don't want to talk about it

You know I can't stand goodbyes

If I asked you to stay

would you take my hand in yours?

Say you'll never leave me

I just need you to know

every day I wish I had said

all the words in my head

It's easier not to get close to you, to stay away from all the hurt. Every time we try this again, it only ends in goodbye. Our sad truth is that we should never have tried.

The night covers my tears, but my heart is still aching after all these years.

Such a sad soul, living in a world you don't belong. I know all those love songs on the radio only remind you of the love that's come and gone. Closing eyes and dreaming of a place where you don't feel so alone.

You must remember that you are human. Filled with thoughts and feelings that will make you ache until the pain feels it might stay. But it is not here to ruin you. The ache is here to remind you that you will survive, in anything you do.

If your heart is missing someone

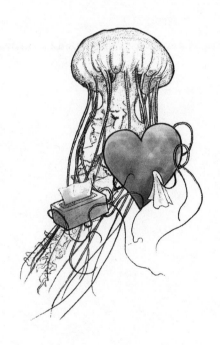

Sometimes I wonder if the people farthest away from us are the people who know us the most. Everyone seems to think that love like this doesn't exist with distance. But then they don't read their emails late at night, speaking to you in secret coded words. They don't see you in the mornings when you've left the laptop running, and there you are, asleep on the other side of the screen.

And then there's all that you are.

A woman with dewdrops in your hair, and a runaway smile, and eyes brighter than diamonds, and the only thing I can think about is that I bet you smell like coffee on a Sunday morning.

I've never really been good at much

other than catching planes and writing things down

So if I were to board a plane and find myself in your city

I hope you might let me write some things across your skin

Like my name and my thoughts

and a few reasons why I'd board that plane again and again

I miss you every day

But today

it feels like everything

I do

is just here to remind me

I am living without you

My hand reaches across the sheets for you

even though I know you're not here

How do you leave me breathless

from miles away

I've never really been jealous of anything, except maybe people with fast cars. But every day I find myself jealous of the things that make up your day. I'm jealous of the coffee you drink, because it has the taste of your lips. I'm jealous of your pillow at night, because it holds all your secrets. I'm jealous of all your blankets, because they're tangled up in you. I'm jealous of the stars outside your window, because they get to watch you sleep. I'm jealous of all your distractions, because they have your time over me. I'm jealous of the things that keep you awake, because lately I don't think they're me. But more than anything, I'm jealous of your 6 a.m., because it'll never tell you how perfect you look, when you just wake up.

Find the kind of love that doesn't make you question their intentions. Find the kind of love that makes the distance between you worth it.

Even if we never see each other again, know that in the moments we held each other's hearts, you were what I needed most.

Our days are full of I miss you and I miss you too texts, counting down months until we are together again. But when we kissed for the first time, I knew all the missing would be worth the taste of your soul.

Sometimes I worry that I won't find someone. That the person who deserves all this love I have to give is out there with someone else. I worry that I won't find a love to believe in, that I won't find a hand that fits with mine. I don't know how I can miss someone I've never met, but I do.

I was so sure that we would be, how am I supposed to accept that now we will never be?

We're not together anymore

You say each time I ask how you are

I'm sorry that I've been calling

And asking about your mom

I've just been wondering how she is

I'm sorry about your dog

I know you loved him a lot

I know it's none of my business

All the things that are happening

In your life

But I still care

I just want to tell you I still love you

But you'll just reply with

"That's not fair."

I felt like a book that you had marked with all your favorite pages. Our love was a story that knew no boundaries. But you lost the book and unmarked all the pages, and now I'm missing our story.

I'm tired of all the texting

Of all the late-night calls

I'm tired of the constant

Wanting

And time feeling like walls

I need your breath on my skin

Your body asleep next to mine

I can't keep pretending I don't miss you

And that I'm fine

I see home in your eyes

But home is so far away

I miss the way you let your hair down

How it fell over your shoulders

It reminded me of the way light spills

From the moon

I'm running every light

chasing after you

I'm watching every sunrise

but they're not as beautiful as you

I know we're only young

but I want you to be mine

My heart is in disguise

all these lost dreams and lies

Because I just want you to feel

the way I do about you

We had skipped school to sit on the hood of your car and drink cherry cola. We were listening to music, the same songs we danced to at the parties thrown when parents weren't home. We talked about getting older, about college and all the dreams we had, if we'd eat more pizza and live in a world that made us feel less alone. You went quiet for a while, as you looked out at the view. And then you said, "I hope in five years, I still know you." Now it's five years later, and I haven't seen you in months. How I miss that cherry cola, and all the dreams we had.

When I think about time, I think of how quickly it passes. I think of all the things we could have done with our time and all the days and weeks I was yours and you were mine. The first time I met you, we were only neighbors, and I know my memory is a little faded, but from that moment my love for you has never wavered. Time has moved on since that memory, and we have all these new ones to share. Some of them are beautiful, some are ugly, some don't even seem fair. I think about all our trials, our road trips, festivals, and the nights spent talking about our future. Somewhere along the way we lost ourselves and lost each other. To be without you is an ache, a feeling of seeing you in all things and every color. I know we have our own journeys, our demons to fight, but I wanted you to know I think of you and us almost every night. Even if we are apart, I grow for you and I know that you grow for me too. Because in the end I know that you are the most beautiful girl I have ever seen, and all I want for us is to be together again.

I wear your sweaters when you're at work all day because they smell like you. And when you come home and cannot find them it's because I am hiding them. Always afraid I won't have another to wear when I miss you.

The exact moment, I couldn't be sure

when we went from friends to something more

Just like I couldn't tell you

the moment it all fell apart

and you left this absence in my heart

You said my arms were the walls to your home

So why when I ask you to come home

You don't?

The distance will close one day

There will be no more interference on the phone

no more waking up at your noon

no more sitting on my balcony wishing I had you

to share the beauty of the moon

You won't be there

and I won't be here

We'll be together

Nothing makes me happier than the arrival gate
and nothing makes me sadder than the departure gate

Distance often gives you a reason to love harder

The odds are against us

stacked all the way to the sky

Our friends tell us to let go

but we can't and we both know

Why

We're in love

even with the miles between us

But the way you make me feel

makes it enough

She drove sixteen hours just for a kiss

Because her lips were what she had missed

When we were sixteen I would come to your window and throw small stones until you opened the curtains. I would climb up the thatch and into your room and we would talk about all we wanted to be. We grew older and went to college and I was still throwing stones and climbing through your window. Until the day I asked you to marry me and you said yes. And I don't know how we went from being in love to strangers, but tonight I stood out on the street and watched the guests arrive to the wedding. But it wasn't our wedding. Because somewhere through the years, I had stopped throwing stones.

It's always

       see you in a month

or

       see you in five days

I can't wait until I can say

       see you tonight

Remember all the plans we made?

Was I naive to think we'd get that far?

Be tender with your forever

The distance is bearable most days. What with being able to call you, text you pictures throughout my day. We can stay up late on video call, I can see your face and smile, we can plan visits in between classes and make playlists to last awhile. But the moment it becomes too hard is when you're sad and I can't hold you.

How to explain

the ache I feel for you

the craving for your touch

the way I miss you

It's in the moments you want to turn to them and share good or bad news that you realize how much of a hole is in your heart when they aren't with you. All you want is for the person you love most to be by your side.

One day our lives won't be filled with boarding passes and weeklong visits. Instead I'll wake up in our apartment and you'll be in the kitchen, sitting at the counter drinking coffee, still wearing my t-shirt from the night before.

We can talk on the phone for hours, burning through conversations the way comets do in the atmosphere. I wish you knew how much I miss you when you're not here. The longing feels like its own universe.

One day I won't have to pack my bags in your room

and watch you cry

wondering when we'll see each other again

There are nights when every goodnight feels like goodbye

All I want

   is to be able to be there

      when you say you need me

I would choose you over sleeping in

I would choose calling you over going out

I would choose your heart

Even before we've had the chance to begin

There is such beauty in patience

as there is pain

But flowers survive

even in the rain

There is great freedom in only having yourself. Not having to worry about supporting anyone else, not having to think or make choices with anyone else in mind. But there is still an ache, some days duller than others, some days not felt until the early hours. It will grasp at you when you think about an achievement and receiving an award and you want someone to be in the corner beaming with pride. You think about it over coffee, when no one is looking at you instead of drinking theirs. In the middle of the night when it's cold and no one is there breathing gently beside you. When you come home and the house is empty, and even if it's peaceful and quiet, you would like to share your thoughts with someone as they set dinner on the table. The freedom to belong to yourself is beautiful, but it's also beautiful to look at someone else and know their favorite moment of the day is when you walk into the room.

If your heart is happy

Appreciate happiness, as it doesn't often stay. But it lives through your smile, your laugh, your deep breaths of relief.

Our first real conversation was on a Ferris wheel. I remember because you were afraid of heights but still came on with me anyway. I could tell you were nervous even as the carnival lights were dancing around us. I told you we would only go around a couple of times, but you said it was okay and that you wanted to stay. I remember asking what you wanted in life and it wasn't weird to be asking you that. I remember you listed all the things I wanted too, with the last being happiness. And I felt the night air as it rushed down my back, wondering how I could possibly ask you to stay when we were only new. But you just looked at me and said, "I know I can be happy with you."

As it rained outside, I listened to the patter on the windowpane and I watched as two raindrops chased each other across the glass. And it reminded me of you, how I would follow you through every season. How we are still us, even if the days don't always stay the same. How I am happy with you, even in the rain.

Don't waste your time with people who bring you down. Bitterness is a disease that gets the better of most people, but that doesn't mean you need to tolerate it. You have flaws just like anybody else. Embrace them, live for them. There is only one you. Forgiveness is happiness. They walk hand in hand. You don't have to forgive everyone in your life. But you do have to forgive yourself.

Every time.

My happiest memories are all of you

If you leave

What am I supposed to do?

Tell me, I want to know

Tell me about the moments that made your hands shake,
tell me about your first kiss and the person who made your
heart break. Tell me what you love to do in your spare time,
tell me about all the places you want to see, about your
favorite books, songs, and flavors of tea. Tell me the thing
that scares you most, tell me the moment you decided who
you are. Tell me the colors that make you dizzy, tell me all the
constellations you know. Tell me the things you hope for, the
wishes you place on stars, tell me the candy that you like, the
flowers that make you sigh. Tell me what makes you breathe,
tell me and I'll never say goodbye.

Darling, I am sorry

I can't act like I don't care

because I do

And your smile

is what I think about

every time

I close my eyes

I could spend hours talking to you and it only feels like a handful of moments. And I know that life can be difficult and challenges get in the way, but with you, life feels effortless. It feels like the struggle is worth it. Just to see you at the end of the day. When I am with you, the sadness goes away.

There isn't a deadline on your body

Firsts are still important; only do what you feel comfortable with

That's happiness, when you make someone feel safe. You are their person. You are the reason they can talk about their deepest secrets. And in a world of constant shaming, you are the one who makes them feel brave to be themselves.

You need to keep moving forward. You cannot get ahead if you refuse to move.

All things serve their purpose and then leave, even happiness. We spend our lives wanting to be happy, and then when it arrives, we are scared to lose it. But if you have to let happiness go, it doesn't mean something else won't come along. In life, there are many things that have purpose, even if sometimes we don't realize it.

Morning Thoughts

When you wake in the morning and you check your phone, I know you're hoping for a good-morning text. They're on your mind right now.

What makes you happy? Climbing bookshelves, roses about to bloom, organizing your desk drawers and cleaning your room. The wind in your hair as you ride your bike, playing the radio loud. Sipping mojitos in the late-night dusk, rising and falling on the chest of someone you love. Swimming in the lake with no school until next week. Achieving your dreams, being with your friends, dancing outside in a snow-filled street. Drinking coffee and watching movies, writing in journals and waiting for the weekend. The things that make you happy are important. If they make you smile and the stress feels lighter, then you deserve to enjoy them. Do what makes you happy.

But you need to stop getting so worked up about things that won't matter a year from now. It is relevant today, yes, but one day it won't be.

Stop punishing yourself for things that will eventually pass.

Happiness is coming home to a freshly made bed. To a house full of scented candles, a glass of wine after the daily struggle. It's walking in the door and hearing the words, "I love you." It's sitting opposite her in your favorite restaurant and hearing,

"I'll support you in everything you do."

You wake up three mornings in a row

and you tell yourself you are not going to make it

But you will

You will

You cannot buy happiness. You cannot boil it down to a few choice words and bottle it away. Happiness is grown from a seed, to a flower, to a forest. Trust your ability to water this seed. Trust the kindness of others and the help from those you hold dearest.

There is just something about early mornings. Awake while everybody else is still asleep. And it feels like you have forgotten the pull of everyday life and you are just a child again, carefree, blowing dandelions in the wind.

Happiness isn't a rush

You don't have to keep up with anyone

Just keep up with yourself

That will do

The energy you put into the world isn't always the same energy you will receive. You could be a ball of light and still be met with people who try to lock you in the dark. What is important is the energy you keep for yourself. Keep the light burning.

To be happy isn't always to be with others. Some of life's greatest thinking is done while we are alone. Other people can't learn to breathe again for you. Other people can't feel or see or hear things in the way you do. Sometimes being happy is stepping away from the things you know. It's breathing in and out and watching your soul grow.

Rushing won't help you in standstill traffic any more than thinking you need to be somebody else will. You have your whole life ahead of you, no matter what age you are. Fill it with things that make you get up in the morning. Fill it with people who support who you want to be.

The sun does not hold all your broken pieces.

It just offers warmth, as you do.

You can be happy and still learn to heal.

You are not emotional or too soft. There are things in life that will try to turn your heart to stone. They will leave you bruised and angry, with feelings you have never known. But to be patient, to feel warmth when people turn cold, is both brave and radiant.

People like to talk about their passions. They like to tell you about the things that make them happy. And you can see the switch, the light that pours out of them when they are speaking of the things they love. Listen to someone when they are talking. Don't shut them down or tell them that their passions don't matter. It's the simplest way to ruin another human being.

In your quest to be understood, don't forget to show humility
don't lose your ability to be understanding

Some chapters don't have happy endings. But you read on anyway, and I think that's the point. Not to be happy all the time but to know the sun always comes back around.

After everything, your heart is still beating and your mind is at peace. You pushed away your demons and you fought back from the shadows. You found happiness even at all your crossroads.

People grow apart. Distance doesn't always mean miles. Sometimes it means two friends going separate ways. The person you poured your heart out to, traveled through new cities with, called at three in the morning just to get ice cream, suddenly becomes someone who can't even text you back. So, you start to wonder what happened and where it all went wrong. How can this person who was once your lifeline now be a stranger who holds all your memories? But people change and become caught up in their own lives. They may not even realize they are doing it. Sometimes friends disappear and we don't know why. But you don't deserve to be ignored. The things you have to say are important; you should never allow someone to make you feel as though they aren't. You should never tolerate someone who can't acknowledge the news you have to share. You don't need this in your life. Let go of people who don't make you happy.

You can't skip chapters, that's not how life works. You have to read every line, meet every character. You won't enjoy all of it. Hell, some chapters will make you cry for weeks. You will read things you don't want to read, you will have moments when you don't want the pages to end. But you have to keep going. Stories keep the world revolving. Live yours, don't miss out.

Make lists when happiness feels far away
Think of the sky turning orange after a hot summer's day
of leaves in the fall
of overgrown sweatshirts and paintings on brick walls
Think of hot chocolate in winter
Think of music and lying in the grass
and things that make your heart beat fast
Think of these things
as you go about your day
Happiness is never really that far away

Happiness won't always be around. There will be days when it feels hidden and nowhere to be found. But your smile keeps the happiness alive, and your laugh too. There is nothing more important than taking care of you.

Sometimes we fall in love with someone's potential. We ignore their behavior because we believe they can be better. But a person doesn't change unless they want to. Your happiness is more important than hanging on to someone else's potential.

When we are happy, we are afraid it will be taken away. That we will wake up one day and the person or moments that made us so happy will disappear. We have spent so long wanting this happiness that when it arrives, we struggle to enjoy it out of fear it will leave. But happiness comes and goes like clouds and rain and steamboats on long rivers. It washes onto the sand and washes back. To find happiness is to navigate through a world that sometimes seems colorless. Happiness is a gift. Enjoy it while it's here.

You taught me not to dwell so much on what was, not to think so much about what will be, but rather live for today with you. Counting each day as a gift, happy to be in love, happy to just be.

It can take weeks or years for broken bones to heal, and some say they've known hearts to be broken for decades. But what is broken is merely cracked. You forget to fill the cracks with light. Let the happiness back into your bloodstream.

You deserve to be cared about

You deserve to be happy

You deserve to be free

You deserve to radiate positive energy

There are just some things not meant for you

but that doesn't mean you won't be happy

In the end our footsteps always lead us

to the things we are meant to do

The world won't always love you for who you are. There are too many bodies here. Too many perceptions of what is and isn't beautiful. So here we are, with most of us uncomfortable in our own skin, wishing to be someone different. Thinking happiness only happens if you fit in. What to do when the world wants you to be prettier, skinnier, curvier, or have lighter or darker skin. You declare your own universe, bright and alive within your veins. You are the king or the queen, the one who makes the rules and ignores everyone who cannot see just how brilliant you are, made from atoms brighter than stars.

These are for your heart

me
her
and our hearts

When someone says
me too
and you realize you are not alone
That the things you have felt
have been felt before
and they will be felt again
You ache, you doubt, you question, you cry
You laugh, you love, and have faith in the sky
me too

Your patience will be tested. You will get frustrated; some days will hurt more than others. But you need to move on from what has already happened, appreciate the things still around you, and embrace the things that are yet to come.

You are a tree and each leaf is a thought,
a word to describe how you are feeling.
But there are too many leaves and fall has
come and gone. So you stand looking to the
sky and asking why you must feel so much.
But if you look around, you will find there are
many other trees with many more leaves.
You must let go of the ache and place a gentle
hand on your heavy heart. Take pride in how much
you've grown, and just remember you are not alone.

We were young and the only thing we listened to was the sound of our hearts racing

I wish for you

the things I wish for myself

Love, strength, and good health

All things in life begin with effort. You are not going to win every moment, but you must still apply the same effort. Do this for yourself.

Not all good people end up with good people.
You can take your time, consider all your choices with logic,
and always do your best. But still your heart can be broken.
Yet good people do survive.
They are always surviving.

Knowing what makes us happy is important. But so is knowing what makes us sad, angry, and anxious. Knowing how to feel is more than distinguishing between emotions. It's also knowing when someone makes you feel like a mountain instead of mere dust and soil.

You are looking for evidence to prove that they don't love you, when there is all this evidence that proves they do. When they hang your sweater in the closet after you come home from work, when they leave you notes on the kitchen counter to have a good day, when you don't feel like cooking so they order pizza.

Someone doesn't have to say "I love you" for it to be true.

I hope you find someone who loves you so fiercely you won't feel the need to cover your face the morning after, afraid for them to see you bare and naked.

Responsibility can feel heavy and growing up too
Some moments feel like nobody understands you
What you are going through
Who to trust
Who you want to be
But in the end, all things come together
you'll see

All things aside
My heart beats for you
Does yours beat for mine too?

There are as many days hope is to be lost as it is to be gained. On the days that you cannot feel this hope, it doesn't mean it's not there.

Your heart is here to grow

water it with love

let the light in

Remember your heart

is a world beating

beneath your skin

We all lose our way,

We take paths we never intended to

We leave our hearts messy

and sometimes we leave the mess

in other people's hearts too

But where there is hope

there is a heart that beats

Please don't give up on yourself

Give me your heart
I will guard it as my own
And give it a home

You are not defined

by the scars on your heart

Let them enrich you

learn from them

Tell others "These are my scars

and I am learning to embrace them"

If you like to dream or think or wear your heart on your sleeve, then do that. People like to tear others down when they are happy, and more so when they're successful. They'll try to find faults because they can't believe the same success isn't happening to them.

You can break your own heart

but you can also heal it

I could give you a million reasons why it's important to keep your heart open, but we'd be here for hours. I could tell you after the darkness the sun always rises, but you know this already. Every battle becomes another story, every scar becomes part of your journey. Your heart is your greatest weapon against turning hard. Keep your heart soft, love without apology.

When the fields grow

My heart swells

Yours for always, just you

You can build happiness. You plant a seed in your heart and let it grow. Let the happiness spread into your arms so when you hold others they feel it. Let it spread into your legs so when you walk people see it in your step. Keep building day by day, until you have an entire empire.

What will make it better she asked

A new day

Whether they stay or go

your heart needs to know

you are stronger for saying no

Each small victory is worth celebrating

The rain clouds return to the sky, as does the sun, the moon, and the stars. Your heart is allowed to cry as much as it is to laugh. Feel what makes your pulse race in the early hours. Good is coming your way soon.

I think you should know
All the love that surrounds you
Everywhere you go

Your heart deserves to take chances, dabble in risk. It deserves to venture out into the world and explore what it does and doesn't love. It deserves to be followed.

There are people out there telling you to be more than beautiful. As if being beautiful doesn't carry its own magic. Beauty is defined as you see fit. If being intelligent, funny, wild, adventurous, and honest is your definition of beautiful, then be beautiful.

Lost love isn't the worst thing you can go through in life. Even if in the moment you feel as though navigating the storm is impossible. The worst thing in life is refusing to evolve from the hurt. Your heart can't grow without you. It needs you in its corner.

In our rib cage lies our heart

Protected

But people can reach inside

and cause chaos

When this happens

remind yourself

You are not a burden

You can't force your heart to feel a certain way. But you can respect people. You can be gentle when letting someone go.

My skin felt raw under your touch
As though my love for you
was far too much

Wherever this life takes us, you will be my greatest memory.
I remember the way you have your coffee and what you look
like in my t-shirts. I remember waking up to the sound of
your footsteps downstairs and falling asleep in your arms.
I remember the way you smell, how you dress for special
occasions, your favorite color, the wall hanging in your
bedroom covered in fairy lights. I remember the curve of your
back and your handwriting, how hard you work for your
dreams. Every memory now shared with mine. I'll remember
you forever.

Some people don't deserve your love. They will take you for granted, toss you aside when it seems easier to be selfish. You need to be strong every time they come knocking. Don't open the door.

People will tell you that the material things given to you hold no value over how your heart feels. But sometimes possessions hold worth, not for the value but for the memories. The small stuffed bear your grandfather gave you before he passed, the necklace left by your mother the day she walked out, the sweater your old love left behind. All things have memories, stories of where they have come from, and they all affect the heart.

You can be passionate and determined and it will still not be enough. You will find a roadblock on every corner, a force pulling you backward instead of forward. You will wonder why someone as passionate as you is going nowhere. But you *are* going somewhere. Every setback is part of the journey. The joy of probability is that eventually something will give. Your determination keeps you in the game.

Sometimes I fall asleep and I am still half awake, watching myself dream. In these moments, I am more than I ever thought I could be. I am more than a dream, more than the moon. I am the universe, and every possibility belongs to me.

Thank you for reading this book.
I hope you enjoyed reading it as much as I enjoyed writing it.

You can view more of my work on Twitter
@CourtPeppernell and Instagram @Courtneypeppernell

Feel free to write to me via courtney@pepperbooks.org

Pillow Thoughts II

Andrews McMeel Publishing
a division of Andrews McMeel Universal
1130 Walnut Street, Kansas City, Missouri 64106

www.andrewsmcmeel.com

18 19 20 21 22 BVG 10 9 8 7 6 5 4 3 2 1

ISBN: 978-1-4494-9508-4

Library of Congress Control Number: 2018934779

Illustrations by Ryan Gerber

Editor: Patty Rice
Designer, Art Director: Diane Marsh
Production Editor: Dave Shaw
Production Manager: Cliff Koehler